HOW TO BUY
Great
SHOES
THAT
FIT

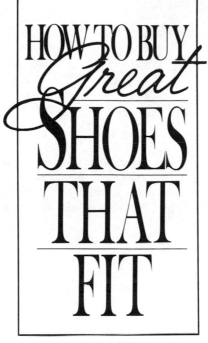

HOW TO BUY *Great* SHOES THAT FIT

SCOTT NORMAN

Illustrations by
David H. Cohen

Prince Paperbacks/Crown Publishers, Inc.   New York

A Prince Paperback

Published by Crown Publishers, Inc., 225 Park Avenue South, New York, New York 10003 and represented in Canada by the Canadian MANDA Group.

Manufactured in the United States of America

Library of Congress Cataloging-in-Publication Data

Norman, Scott.
    How to buy great shoes that fit / by Scott Norman; illustrations by David H. Cohen.
        p.   cm.
    1. Shoes—Purchasing.   I. Title.
TT678.5.N67 1988
646'.3—dc19   88-7010

ISBN 0-517-57048-3

10 9 8 7 6 5 4 3 2 1

First Edition

To Mrs. Ruth A. Carley
Thanks, Mom, for your faith, your help, and your love!

CONTENTS

INTRODUCTION

Shoe Shopping Doesn't Have to Be a Traumatic Experience!

Shoes, shoes, shoes. We love how they look, yet hate how they feel. Many women are so fed up with uncomfortable shoes that they have chosen athletic shoes as an alternative—regardless of how bad they look. But tennis shoes aren't your only option. I've written this book to give you the basic information to walk into any shoe store, select good shoes that really fit, and keep them looking and feeling good for a long time. Being more comfortable in the shoes you wear, spending less money on them, and experiencing less frustration while shoe shopping is what this book is all about.

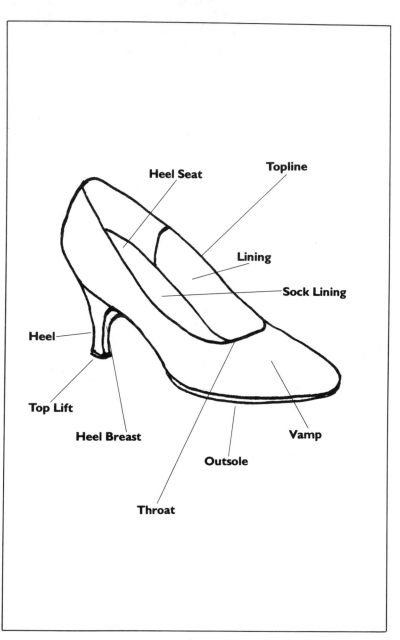

Heel Seat

Topline

Lining

Sock Lining

Heel

Top Lift

Heel Breast

Vamp

Outsole

Throat

A Shoe

1
ANATOMY
OF A SHOE

Parts of a Shoe

Heel breast. The inside part of the heel facing the front of the shoe. This is where heel height is officially measured.

Heel counter. The stiffened piece of material inserted between the outer and inner linings of the upper at that part of the shoe that surrounds your heel. Its purpose is to strengthen the back part of the shoe and keep it from losing its shape while supporting the heel.

Insole. The central part of the shoe (usually leather, felt, cork, fiberboard) formed to the "last," layered between the outsole and the sole of the foot, to which the rest of the shoe is attached. The insole can either be left uncovered or have a sock lining glued to it.

Linings. Referred to by the part of the shoe they cover— sock, vamp, quarter, tongue, back. These layers of leather, fabric, man-made material, or cushioned padding cover the inner part of the shoe and protect the foot from seams, nails, threads, and glue. The sock lining refers to the material that includes the insole, upon which the foot rests. Upper linings help the shoe keep its shape and protect it from stains and deterioration caused by normal perspiration by absorbing moisture from feet and hose.

Quarter. The back half of the shoe's upper, attached to the vamp; it covers the heel counter and sides of the shoe.

Shank, shankpiece. The shank is the middle part of the shoe under the arch of the foot. It is like a bridge, connecting the front and rear parts of the shoe.

Most shoes, especially those with heels, have a reinforced steel shankpiece layered between the outsole and insole. This supports the body's weight.

Throat. The forward edge of the vamp opening facing the instep.

Toe box. Stiffened material that forms a "roof" over the toes. It maintains the shape of the front of the shoe and protects the foot.

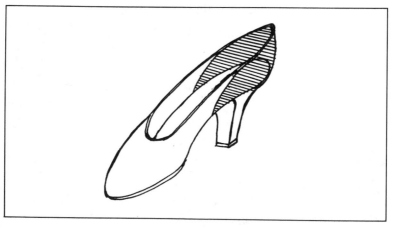

Heel Counter

Topline. The uppermost rim or edge of the shoe, farthest away from the sole, into which the foot is inserted.

Upper. Those parts of the shoe above the insole and outsole (the quarter, vamp, counter, and linings).

Vamp. The front part of the shoe's upper; it covers the toes from the ball of the foot forward.

Miscellaneous Terms

Construction. The method of attaching the upper to the sole by welting, stitching, vulcanizing, cementing, or nailing.

Embossing. A stamped or engraved pattern on the surface of leather or other material made by a special machine using heavy pressure. Usually done in patterns resembling animal hides or exotic reptile skins.

Filler. A layer of felt, cork, or other material found between the insole and outsole of the shoe; it helps to cushion the sole.

Gusset. A piece of elastic, usually hidden at the calf of a boot, to which are sewn strips of leather that match the boot, thus enabling the boot to expand at the calf without detracting from its appearance.

Inlay. A contrasting piece of material or leather, inserted under an opening in the upper to decorate the shoe.

Kiltie. A folded, slashed fringe flap found on the vamp of sport shoes. Sometimes used on an oxford to cover the lace.

Last. A plastic, wooden, or metal form, shaped somewhat like a foot, over which the shoe is made. Separate lasts are required for left and right feet, and for each different style, heel height, and size of a shoe.

Wing-Tip Shoe

Lasting margin. A piece of upper leather that is tucked in between the insole and the outsole of the shoe and then tacked, stitched, or glued down.

Overlay. A piece of contrasting or harmonizing material stitched to a part of the upper as decoration or trim.

Perforation. Small holes, often round, but sometimes square, oval, or diamond-shaped, which are punched into the upper surface of the shoe.

Spectator. A shoe of two different colors.

Wing-tip. An M-shaped pattern, often perforated, which covers the vamp. Often mistakenly called a spectator. (See illustration above.)

Size Measurements

Arch measurement. The measurement of the foot, last, and shoe *from the heel to the joint of the big toe.* It is extremely important in determining the size shoe you should wear.

Length measurement. The measurement of the foot, last, and shoe *from the heel to the end of the longest toe.*

Width measurement. The side-to-side measurement across the ball of the foot. On a last, and subsequently a shoe, the width measurement is really the *girth* (circumference) of the shoe at its widest part.

Upper Materials

Listed here are the most common materials used as shoe uppers today.

Leathers. Leather remains the Cadillac of shoe upper materials. Made of animal skins and hides, it is lightweight, strong, durable, and tear-resistant. It keeps the foot cool by breathing, letting air circulate while allowing moisture to escape from the shoe. Leather also absorbs moisture, drawing perspiration away from the foot. Because it is so supple, leather stretches and conforms to the shape of the foot and becomes softer with use.

Leather is available in a wide range of colors and finishes, has a luxurious texture and feel, and is capable of extensive detailing. Leather signifies a quality shoe in a wide range of prices.

On the negative side, leather is less durable and harder to clean than man-made materials.

The most common leathers used in women's shoes are:

Calfskin. Tanned from the skin of young cows or calves, it is one of the highest quality leathers. Calfskin has a fine grain, is strong, yet soft and supple, but does not stretch out of shape. It is lightweight, porous, scuff-resistant, and polishes well.

Cowhide (side leather). The hide of a grown cow is used not only for uppers but also for linings and other shoe components. Cowhide comes in many weights, thicknesses, and finishes: smooth, brushed (suede), patent, or embossed. It is supple, porous, and molds to the foot well.

Suede. Suede refers to a finish, *not* to a particular type of leather. It is made by buffing or sandpapering the flesh or underside of an animal skin (kid, calf, cowhide, split leather, or pigskin) to create a velvetlike pile or nap surface that is soft to the touch and extremely comfortable to wear. A few words of caution about suede: It often stretches out of shape, and unlined suede shoes may "crock" or bleed some of the dye onto your hose when your feet perspire. It can also be difficult to clean.

Other suedelike materials include brushed leather, which is often a split leather that has been buffed. Its nap is somewhat coarse and not as fine as suede. Nubuck is another leather whose outer surface (grain) is softly buffed to appear like buckskin. It has a very fine nap that can barely be felt.

Kidskin. Tanned from skins of young or mature goats. It is lightweight, very porous, pliable, soft, and very strong for its weight. Kidskin is also durable, scuff-resistant, and accepts colored dyes extremely well.

Patent leather. Produced from leathers that are varnished or coated with a film of urethane resin to give them a high-gloss, mirrorlike finish. Patent is flexible, waterproof, soil- and scuff-resistant, and generally lasts a long time. Because it is coated with resin, it does not breathe. It also does not stretch as easily as other leathers.

Split leather. Made from thick cattle hides that have been split into two or more pieces. It is used for uppers in inexpensive shoes as well as shoe linings and insoles. It is commonly buffed to create a suedelike surface, although it is often used for smooth, embossed, and patent leathers, too. It is lightweight, flexible, strong, and durable.

Exotic Leathers. Exotic leathers such as alligator, crocodile, lizard, snakeskin, and ostrich are tanned from the hides and skins of these reptiles and birds. They're expensive because of their distinctive surface characteristics, the difficulty in obtaining them, and the limited quantity available. They are usually very strong, durable, and scuff-resistant, though not as supple as calf or kidskin.

Alligator. One of the highest quality exotic skins. It is tanned from the hides of small- to medium-size alligators found all over the world. It has a very high-gloss finish, usually tanned in deep, rich colors. Its distinctive grain pattern appears as etched squares or tiles. It is scuff-resistant, extremely durable, and quite expensive.

Crocodile. Similar to alligator in appearance and wear qualities, yet differs in that some of its scales can have follicles that appear to be clusters of small pinpoints. It too is extremely durable, scuff-resistant, and very expensive.

Lizard. Made from the skin of several species of lizards found in the tropical environments of South America and Southeast Asia. It is a tough skin, characterized by small oval, circular, diamond, or rectangular patterns. It is durable, scuff-resistant, flexible, and fairly expensive.

Ostrich. The only shoe leather that is taken from a bird. It comes from ranches on which these birds are specially raised. The skin has a prominent nubbed surface dotted by quill holes that once held feathers. It is extremely strong and durable, yet soft, supple, lightweight, and usually won't dry out or crack.

Snakeskin. Made from many varieties of snakes that come from Asia, Africa, and South America. It has a scaly surface, and although very lightweight, it is very strong. Some skins are characterized by unique surface designs. Snakeskin, while a beautiful, luxurious skin, may not be practical for an everyday shoe because its scales nick easily and fray with wear.

Man-made (Synthetic) Materials. Man-made materials are low-cost leather substitutes that sometimes perform better than leather since they're virtually indestructible, clean easily, and are weather-resistant. They can also be finished to look like any type of leather or exotic skin.

The disadvantages of synthetics are:
- They don't breathe (absorb or pass moisture), which means they'll be hot and moist, especially in closed shoes and boots.
- They have memory retention, which causes them to return to their original shape rather than molding permanently to the foot. Because of this, they must fit perfectly to begin with.
- They are not as flexible as leather.

Why Are Shoes So Expensive?

In recent years, the price of shoes has increased tremendously. This is due in part to the decline in the strength of the U.S. dollar, continuing worldwide demand for leathers, and the escalating costs of materials used to make shoes. These result in higher costs to manufacturers, who pass them along to the retailer and are eventually paid for by the consumer.

What goes into the cost of a pair of shoes?

Materials. The most costly element in a pair of shoes is the upper material. Leather uppers, more costly than synthetics, can mean the difference between a pair of shoes that costs $30 and one that costs $80. Better leathers—kidskin, calfskin, exotics—are naturally more expensive than cowhide or other lesser quality leathers. Additionally, you will pay more for the quantity of material used to make different types of shoes (pumps versus sandals), shoes with metallic or other special finishes, shoes with leather linings versus those that are unlined or lined with synthetic materials, shoes with leather soles.

Workmanship. Machine-made shoes are relatively easy to make and less expensive because less time and labor are used to make them. Hand operations (appliqués, perforations, and underlays) require specialized craftsmanship and attention to detail that are more time-consuming and therefore more costly.

Designer or brand name. Many high-fashion styles originate with "name" designers and consequently are more expensive. Top designers are often first on the market with new, innovative styles, using advanced colors and better leathers. They also "sell" (license) their names to shoe manufacturers, which boosts the price.

Designer labels and brand names imply quality. These companies put their reputation on the line every time they put their name on their shoes, and therefore you can usually expect a better quality shoe.

Costs of running a business. These are of course reflected in the final price of your shoes. Salespeople working for commissions (you pay more for skilled, experienced, better-trained salesmen), the decor of the store, liberal return policies, advertising, and store location are all paid for by you, the consumer, in the mark-up on the product.

Signs That Indicate a "Quality" Shoe

**"Quality Is Remembered
Long after Price Is Forgotten."**

Here are some quality checkpoints you should look for when shopping for shoes.

- Buckles should be smooth and have no rough edges.
- Buckles on strap shoes should be attached with a piece of elastic.
- The topline should be finished off so there are no rough edges or loose threads.
- The upper edge of the topline should be dyed the same color as the rest of the upper.
- Eyelets on lace-up shoes (oxfords) should be reinforced with metal grommets for easier lacing.
- Soles should be flexible to enable the foot to bend with a minimum of effort.
- The heel counter should extend toward the front of the shoe, be lined with suede at the back, be somewhat stiff to keep its shape, and have a very thin back to grasp and support the heel.
- The back seams of the heel counter should be straight.
- Sock linings of open-toe or open-back shoes should be dyed to match the rest of the shoe.
- Better shoes have full-leather sock linings. Shoemakers often cut costs by using half-leather sock linings or those made of synthetics. Leather sock linings are better because they breathe and absorb moisture, which lessens bacteria, fungal diseases, and foot odor often caused by perspiration and exacerbated by sock linings made of synthetic materials.
- Padded sock linings greatly add to your comfort.
- Linings should be smooth, not wrinkled.

- Suede shoes should always be lined to keep the dye from rubbing off onto your hose.
- Fabric evening shoes should be fully lined to keep them from stretching too easily and to prevent the upper from becoming stained.
- Better quality shoes usually come in a greater variety of lengths and widths.
- Leather soles are considered the best material because they are lightweight, resist punctures, bend easily with a minimum of effort, and are excellent insulators of heat and cold. Shoes with genuine leather soles will often have an imprint on the bottom of the sole in the shape of a hide denoting that it is leather. NOTE: Some soles have this stamp but read "leather upper, *man-made* sole."
- The finer the stitching (more stitches per inch), the better the workmanship. A shoe with more stitches holds the material better, whereas fewer stitches often let a seam pucker or separate.
- Stitching sewn too close to the edge of a seam, thread knots not finished properly, broken threads, and broken outer stitching all indicate inferior quality.
- Straps should be lined, cemented, and sewn together. There should not be any rough edges and straps that buckle should have from six to eight holes punched in them.
- Top lifts should be serrated so you don't slip when walking.
- The upper should be free of glue spots or other marks. The color and texture of the upper should be uniform. There shouldn't be any glue showing where the upper meets the sole.
- The upper should be made of a soft material (preferably leather) that is comfortable and easily accommodates the irregularities of the foot.
- Better quality shoes are lightweight, causing less strain on feet and legs.

HOW TO BE A SMART SHOE SHOPPER

Shoe-Shopping Tips

Shop When You Have Sufficient Time. Many costly mistakes have been made by people who allow themselves only a few minutes to shop. Shopping for shoes between errands, during your lunchtime, or just before store closing does not allow you time to try on different styles, compare sizes, and, *most important,* walk about the department to make sure both shoes fit properly.

Don't Shop When Your Feet Hurt. Shopping for shoes when your feet hurt does not allow you to accurately judge whether a shoe fits or not. You won't be able to tell whether the discomfort you are feeling is from the new shoe or from the shoes you wore into the store.

Don't Wear Thongs When You Are Looking for High Heels. In other words, avoid shopping for one type of shoe when you have been walking all day long in a totally different style. Not only will you shock your feet trying on shoes, but you probably won't be wearing the right clothing either, and the look you want will be difficult to visualize.

Don't Shop with People Who Will Distract You. Avoid bringing along friends, children, or others who could interrupt your shopping.

Wear or Bring Appropriate Hosiery with You. Try to wear the type, color, and thickness of hosiery (sheer or opaque hose, socks) that you will wear with the shoes you are looking for. By wearing the right hose, you will be able to assess correctly the feel, look, color, and fit of the shoes. During the summertime, when you tend to go barelegged, bring along a pair of knee highs with you.

Bring Any Inserts or Pads That You Wear in Your Shoes. If you wear any kind of arch support, metatarsal pad, heel pad, orthotic, or insole, be sure to bring these with you, since putting *anything* in your shoes changes how they fit.

Bring Color-Compatible Clothing or Swatches with You. Many women never think of matching shoes to an outfit until they are already shopping. If you can't wear the outfit, bring a fabric swatch or an accessory with you when you shop so you can purchase a shoe that is coordinated with your outfit.

Shop for Shoes at Midafternoon. The best time of day to fit your feet is midafternoon. Because feet tend to swell throughout the day, you don't want to fit them in the morning when they are at their smallest or in the evening when they are at their largest.

If you must shop for shoes early in the day, take into

consideration how much your feet swell and allow for this when they're being fitted.

NOTE: **It's always better to buy a shoe that is bigger rather than smaller.** The bigger shoe can always be padded to take up extra space but, the smaller, tighter shoe can't always be stretched.

Try to Buy Shoes during the Season You'll Wear Them. It's difficult to judge fit when shopping for shoes months before you'll actually be wearing them. Shopping for summer shoes when it's cold outside is difficult because your feet are smaller in the winter than they'll be in the summer. (And vice versa.)

The key to buying fall/winter shoes or boots properly during the summer: Shop very early in the day before your feet have had a chance to swell. And, when shopping for spring/summer shoes during the winter, shop at the very end of the day when your feet are at their largest, so they'll be closer to the size they'll be during the summer.

Communicate Clearly with Your Salesperson. If the shoes you're trying on don't feel quite right, tell your salesperson exactly what you're feeling and at what part of your foot. If you can be more specific than "they just don't feel right," a salesperson, familiar with fitting feet, can take this information and use his or her experience to search for the right last, size, or style, or perhaps adjust the shoe where needed.

Don't Let a Salesperson Intimidate You. Remember, you are the one with the money. Don't ever feel you have to buy something, no matter how much time the salesperson has spent with you. If the shoe fits you and you want to buy it, fine. But don't buy something just because you find it hard to say no. On the other hand, don't lead the salesperson on if you are just browsing.

Before Signing on the Dotted Line, always check the pair of shoes you're buying for nicks, scuff marks, and the like. Shoes can be tried on many times, or even bought and returned, before you finally buy them. Often they are tossed around and scratched in the process. You'll also want to check the inside of the shoe for sharp edges, thread knots, glue, wrinkled linings, or nails that are sticking up. If you find something you don't like, ask for another pair. If that's not possible, ask to have the shoes fixed. Perhaps they'll give you a discount.

Also, check to make sure you have both a right and left shoe of the same size. I've seen many customers over the years who have taken home mismatched pairs.

Finally, ask about the store's return policy *before* you pay.

Test Your New Shoes at Home

This is where you can avoid adding to the shoe graveyard already sitting in your closet. Even if you are sure the shoes fit, give them at least one more test at home before wearing them outside. Most shoe stores, as a rule, do not take back shoes once they have been worn outside. It is for this very reason that you should **never** wear a pair of new shoes out of the store after you have bought them, even if you are convinced they are perfect.

I have heard so many women comment that their shoes never feel as good outside of the store as they do when they first try them on. The reason for this is so simple, yet most women are unaware of it. Few shoes are tested *thoroughly* enough before they are worn outside, and by then it's usually too late to return them if they're not comfortable. Below are several tips you should follow before wearing your new shoes outside.

Walk on a Hard-Surface Floor. People who design shoe stores are shrewd. Most shoe departments are well carpeted.

But how many carpeted sidewalks have you seen lately? Walking on carpeting can leave you unsure of how comfortable your new shoes are going to be once you're on sidewalks and streets. Therefore, testing your new shoes on a hard surface is a *must* before deciding to keep them. Spend some time walking on tile, wood, or some other hard-surface floor so you'll get an idea of how your shoes will feel once you really "wear" them. This won't mar the bottom of the shoes if you protect them beforehand. With some surfaces (like vinyl) you may not have to protect the soles at all, but if you need to, it can be done in several ways. Models who borrow shoes for fashion shows put masking tape on the soles. Even though the tape may remove the top layer of the varnish when you pull it off, it leaves the rest of the sole in excellent condition. You can also put a pair of socks or a cloth shoe bag over the shoes. You may not have to do this, but it will eliminate the risk of being unable to return the shoes if they don't fit. However, if you *do* mar the soles of the shoes when testing them and decide that they aren't right for you, most shoe repairmen are capable of refinishing the soles for a nominal fee.

Walk as Hard and as Fast as You Do Normally. In the store, most women merely amble up to the nearest mirror, look at the shoes for a few moments, and then sit back down. If you walk at a slow pace, then this is fine. But if you are like most women, who walk hard and fast in their shoes, you must give new shoes the same kind of testing. So whether you are trying on shoes in the store or at home, you must really **walk** in them before deciding to keep them.

Bringing your new shoes home first, and not wearing them from the store, is wise on several other counts: It gives you a chance to try them on with all your outfits, to decide if you really love the shoes, and to test them properly for comfort—not just that day, but a few days later.

TIPS FOR SHOPPING SALES

- Make a list of what you need before you go into the store, and stick to that list.
- Don't buy shoes on sale just because they're a bargain. You should be asking yourself, "Do I need them?" rather than "How much am I saving?"
- Always try on both shoes. Most stores only put right shoes out to try on. Unfortunately, most people's left feet are larger than their right and this larger foot is the one that must be tested for comfort.
- Make sure to test the shoes thoroughly before buying them. Most mark-down shoes are sold as "final sale."
- It usually pays to shop on the first day of the sale, even though you may have to fight the crowds. In fact, if you can wait in line before the store opens, do so. You'll be one of the first customers to be waited on and receive the best selection of shoes before they've been picked over.
- Hold on to the display shoe. Most stores put a right shoe on the rack and if two customers want the same shoe, usually the one who has possession of the right shoe is entitled to the pair.

Where Are You Most Likely to Find a Good Salesperson?

The right salesperson, one who is knowledgeable, patient, and honest, with whom you can discuss fit and shoe care, is worth his weight in gold. He is likely to be found at independent and specialty shoe stores selling better and more expensive shoes and you will probably pay for this added service. Usually, the last place to expect quality service is at a department store or discount shoe store.

A PLEA FROM THE SHOE SALESPERSON

The points listed below can determine the type and quality of service you receive from a salesperson. Most salespeople become irritated with or are reluctant to wait on customers who

- Interrupt a salesperson who is waiting on another customer.
- Show a lack of respect for the store's merchandise.
- Bad-mouth the store's products or policies.
- Send the salesperson back to the stockroom for many pairs of shoes, one at a time.
- Send their salesperson back to the stockroom several times for different shoes and then end up not buying anything.
- Don't buy a shoe that the salesperson has spent extra time calling other stores to find.
- Constantly return shoes.
- Shop in a hurry.
- Have the salesperson hold shoes they have no intention of coming back for.
- Walk into the store wearing athletic or orthopedic-looking shoes.

When Are You Entitled to Return a Worn Pair of Shoes?

"Legitimate" Defects. Here are "legitimate" damages or defects that should allow you to return a pair of worn shoes for credit, exchange, or repair.

Broken heels. A heel should last the life of the shoe unless unusually stressed or abused.

Heel lifts that come off the shoe. The shoe store should take these in without any questions and send them in to be repaired without charge.

Detached shoe ornaments should be replaced free of charge.

Broken shankpiece. The shankpiece of your shoes should not break unless subjected to extreme stress. You'll know if the shankpiece is broken because you'll either hear a clicking sound or the shoe will bounce and sag while you walk.

Sole separation is a manufacturer's defect that should be repaired by the shoe store unless the shoes were bought too tight, are worn continually (therefore never allowed to dry out), or are quick-dried. Unless abused, sole separation should not happen to a quality shoe.

Squeaky shoes. Squeaks are usually found at the heel (possibly a broken shankpiece) and in the sole. A shoe will squeak when two pieces of dry material (such as cork or leather) rub against each other within the shoe. A shoe repairman usually can fix a squeaky sole. But, since this shouldn't happen in the first place, it should be the responsibility of the shoe store to take care of the problem.

Wrinkled linings. Lined shoes indicate better quality and these linings should not be wrinkled. This is sloppy workmanship and can quite easily irritate your foot.

Rough seams inside a shoe, such as tongue or vamp seams, can irritate your foot and tear your hosiery.

Dye that rubs off onto your hosiery is often a result of unlined suede shoes and should entitle you to a new pair of shoes.

"Nonlegitimate" Defects. Below are listed what many people mistakenly believe to be returnable "defects," but aren't.

Unfinished thread knots. These can tear a hole in your hose, but even though it is shoddy workmanship, it is not a defect that will lead to the shoe falling apart. You can easily fix these by filing the knot down with an emery board. If you run your hose on knotted threads, you may be justified in asking the store to reimburse you for the cost of your ruined hose.

TIPS IF YOU NEED TO RETURN A PAIR OF WORN SHOES

If you must return a pair of shoes you've worn only *slightly* because they're "killing" your feet, first take them to a shoe-repair shop and have the soles refinished to look like new. Usually a store's only concern is that they be able to resell the shoe, so many retailers will take back a shoe that has been worn *minimally* as long as it looks new (few creases across the vamp and a sole that looks unworn). In addition,

- Bring them in *as soon* as you notice something is wrong.
- If you feel you have been misfit by the salesperson, be prepared to explain why you feel justified in returning the shoes (the salesperson said they'd stretch, for instance).
- Bring all of your receipts with you.
- Don't make any damages worse. ("Damages" made worse are very obvious to those who deal with shoes daily.)
- Call the store beforehand to find out who has the authority to take back worn shoes. This will be the person you want to speak with.
- You will be given more leeway in returning a pair of worn shoes if you are a charge-card customer, you spend a lot of money in the store, or you bought them from a department store.
- If you feel the shoe store is being unreasonable and all else fails, take the matter up with your Better Business Bureau.

Nicked or scuffed heels or toes. Many women come into the store complaining about a piece of leather on the heel or toe of their shoe that "mysteriously" peeled or came off. It's really no mystery at all. We all unknowingly kick or run into things with our shoes. Although it's frustrating, this isn't a "defect."

Heel lifts that wear down quickly. This is something that occurs naturally on shoes with narrow heels, since much of the body's weight is concentrated onto this very small area at the base of the heel. Unfortunately, they do wear down quickly and should be replaced often.

Split back seams. The back seam of a shoe will sometimes split if you force your foot into the shoe without using a shoehorn.

Many shoe stores expect to be given the opportunity to repair a worn, though defective, shoe, first, before they make an exchange or give credit to the customer. Much depends upon how soon after the purchase the shoe develops a problem, and the decision is usually at the discretion of the department or store manager.

Repairs Your Shoe Store Should Be Able to Do for You

The shoe store you bought your shoes from should take responsibility for minor repairs, padding, and stetching as long as it is within a "reasonable" period of time after the purchase. Depending upon the quality and cost of the shoe, four to five months is a fair period of time to expect the store to take care of such repairs. Below are listed repairs and adjustments that your shoe store should be able to help you with.

Boot Repairs. Some shoe stores are able to stretch the calves or instep area of a boot.

Minor Fitting Aids. You can improve the fit of your shoes with tongue pads, pinch pads, heel pads and other fitting aids.

Tongue pads. Used in lace-up shoes to take up excess space and keep your heel from slipping.

Pinch pads. Used inside the shoe at places that bind, cut, or pinch the foot, often at the edge of the toe box, where the shoe flexes.

Heel pads. Used to lift an irritated area of the foot above the topline of the shoe to avoid blisters or calluses.

Ball pads (jimmies or halters). A shoe store can easily fix a shoe that slips in the heel by placing a pad underneath the ball of the foot.

Glue jobs. Gluing down loose sock linings.

Hole punching. Adding extra holes to shoes with straps.

Shoe Stretching. The following is a list of stretches that many shoe stores can do for you.

Lifting the vamp, softening or crimping the throat at the waist/instep.

Softening the edges of the topline, breaking out the heel counter, or filing down any sharp edges.

Spot stretching to accommodate irregular toes, bunions, corns, hammertoes.

Stretching the width of the entire shoe.

Lifting the height of the toe box.

IS IT REALLY NECESSARY TO "BREAK IN" NEW SHOES?

Nobody likes to break in new shoes, but to a certain degree it is necessary. A leather shoe—bought slightly snug and not tight—shouldn't cause you any discomfort when you break it in. (It's when you buy shoes that are tight and expect them to stretch that you run into trouble.) Leather shoes mold to the feet as heat and moisture cause the leather to break down slightly and change shape according to the contours of the foot.

. . . .

Tips for breaking in new shoes

- Wear new shoes for only a few hours at a time. Gradually increase the amount of wearing time so the shoe molds to your foot slowly.
- Spray the inside front part (the vamp) of your shoes with liquid shoe stretch before you wear them for the first time. You can buy this at most shoe-repair shops.
- Flex the soles of the shoes a few times before wearing them.

How Much Will My Shoes Stretch?

It's impossible to say how much a shoe will stretch. A leather shoe is only going to stretch what the leather itself will allow, not what the repairman, salesperson, or customer wants it to. Certain parts of every skin are more pliable than others, and it's hard to tell how much each will stretch without the material or a seam splitting.

The following guidelines should help you determine how much to expect a shoe to stretch.

What Is the Upper Made Of? Man-made uppers will only temporarily mold to your feet as your body heat warms them up. Once you remove them, they quickly return to their original shape. It's advisable to buy these shoes with a perfect fit. Leather, on the other hand, molds more immediately and permanently. How quickly leather molds to the foot depends upon its quality. Suede stretches more readily than other materials. Fabric uppers made of canvas and linen also mold to the foot quickly, as do woven or mesh fabrics. Exotic leathers stretch very little if at all. But a snakeskin shoe (usually leather-lined) molds to the foot much like a regular leather shoe does.

Is the Shoe Lined or Unlined? A lined shoe (two sheaths of material) takes longer to mold to your foot than an unlined model (one sheath of material), which molds to the foot almost immediately.

Is the Shoe "Snug" or "Tight"? A snug shoe will comfortably mold to your foot over time and can be easily spot-stretched if need be. A "tight" shoe is one that hurts, pinches, or cramps the foot and should *not* be bought under any circumstances—even it it's made of good leather. By the time this shoe is broken in, it will be your feet that have been transformed to another shape, not your shoes!

A fleshy foot can sometimes be fit more snuggly in a shoe than a thin, bony foot, because the fleshy foot has more padding to withstand pressure while the bony foot has almost none.

If Snug, Where? A shoe will stretch only if it is snug at the widest part of the foot (the ball) or its immediate area. Your toes should not be confined from the middle of the vamp forward, because shoes do not stretch here and *cannot* be stretched.

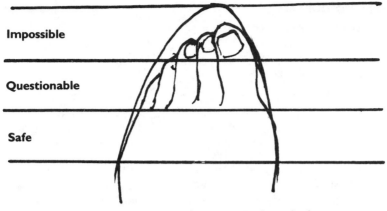

Impossible

Questionable

Safe

Where a Shoe Can and Cannot Be Stretched

What Time of Day Do You Buy Your Shoes? If you buy shoes at the beginning of the day, make sure to allow extra space for your feet to swell later on. If you buy your shoes snug before your feet have had a chance to swell, they will probably be tight later on in the day after your feet have swollen.

Should You Buy Your Shoes Tight Expecting Them to Stretch? Definitely *not*. You shouldn't have to go through the transitional stages of tight, good fit, and then sloppy. Buying a shoe tighter than is comfortable and expecting it to stretch is a bad idea. Shoes stretch in direct proportion to the amount of pressure that is being exerted upon them by your feet. If you buy your shoes on the tight side they will stretch a lot because your feet are exerting a lot of pressure on them. A shoe that is bought slightly snug or perfect to begin with endures less stress and thus stretches less.

The exception to this is an unconstructed, unlined leather shoe that can be bought snugger than normal. If bought with a perfect fit, these can end up stretching out of shape.

WARDROBE TIPS

The following are some tips you can use to buy shoes that will be most flattering for your foot, leg, and body type.

- Use a full-length mirror when trying on new shoes. Then when you get home, do so again. This time, try them on with the clothing you'll be wearing them with, looking at whether the shoes complement your clothing and figure.

- Never look straight down on the shoes you're trying on. They'll look like boats if you do! Nobody looks at your shoes from this angle and you shouldn't either. Look at them from a distance, because this is how everyone else will view them.

- Choose shoes that are darker than or the same color as the clothing you are wearing. These usually blend in better with the clothing you wear. Also, if you don't want your shoes or feet to attract attention, wear dark-colored shoes. They won't stand out as much as bright or light colors.

- Blend or contrast? Wearing a shoe the same color of your leg or stocking continues the lines of the leg and makes them appear longer (which is good if you have large legs, thick ankles, or big feet). A shoe that contrasts with your leg divides the body, legs, and feet, which is good if your feet are narrow or your legs are thin.

What Kind of Stretching Can Be Done to a Shoe? If a shoe has to have major stretching, it was probably the wrong size, style, or last to begin with. The only kind of stretching I advocate, for a properly fitted shoe, is spot stretching, which creates a small pocket in the material for a protruding toe, bunion, or some other sore spot. Lifting the toe box can also be done, but this usually indicates a shoe bought too short or of the wrong last for your shape foot.

Boots are difficult to stretch around the vamp and instep. They can be eased some, but major stretching can't always be done. A good leather boot can be stretched around the calf about 1″ or so.

Major stretching deforms a shoe. Stretching should only be used for slight modifications to specific areas of a shoe.

When buying shoes, remember that the worst thing you can do to your feet is to have your shoes exert excess pressure on them. Most foot problems are pressure-induced. It's always better to buy a shoe bigger and have it padded if need be, rather than smaller hoping it will stretch.

Using the tips in this chapter, you should be able to go into a shoe salon and buy comfortable shoes. I guarantee that if you follow the suggestions outlined above, you will spend less time and money shopping for shoes and be much happier with your purchases.

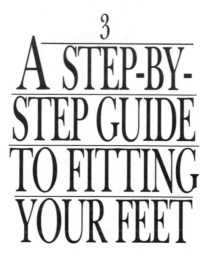

3
A STEP-BY-STEP GUIDE TO FITTING YOUR FEET

I'd like to start by asking you to forget everything you know about fitting your feet. The condition of your feet is in large part a reflection of the way you buy, fit, and wear your shoes. If you're unhappy with the way your feet feel in shoes, why not reevaluate how you are fitting them?

Unless otherwise noted, we'll be talking about pumps in this chapter, since they are the most difficult type of shoes to fit.

The Secret to Fitting Your Feet Comfortably

Your Toes Must Be Free. You must actually be able to wiggle your toes in your shoes while you're *standing*. They should never be pinched or crowded. Feel the sides of the shoe with your fingers. If your toes are bulging out (especially the little toe), then the shoe is too tight and probably too short. If you can't wiggle your toes, you are unnecessarily damaging your feet.

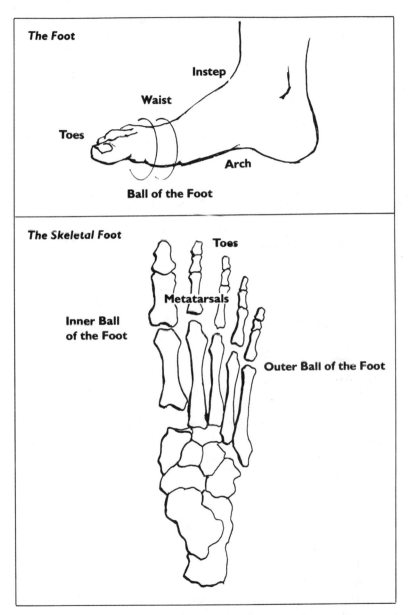

The Foot

Instep

Waist

Toes

Arch

Ball of the Foot

The Skeletal Foot

Toes

Metatarsals

Inner Ball
of the Foot

Outer Ball of the Foot

NOTE: Ball of the foot refers *both* to the metatarsal (base) joint of the big toe *and* to all five metatarsal joints—the *widest* part of the foot.

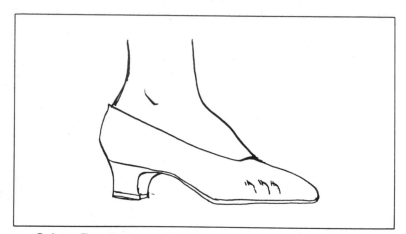

Bulging Toes Indicate a Misfit; Not Enough Space for the Toes

Make sure your shoes have *at least* ½″ to ⅝″ of empty space in front of your *longest toe*. This is especially important in tapered-toe and low-heel shoes because the entire foot stretches forward with each step you take, and if you're not careful they'll be crammed into the end of the shoe when you walk. This isn't as crucial with round-toe, square-toe, or high-heel shoes. You may find yourself able to wear a half size shorter in these styles.

Look for shoes with long vamps even though they tend to be less fashionable. These styles, which are longer from the ball of the foot to the toe, provide much more room for the toes. Unfortunately, many of today's styles have short vamps that allow very little space for the toes, not only in the length, but in the width. This is especially true where the shoe begins to taper. For a tapered-toe shoe to be comfortable, it must have a longer vamp, otherwise the toes will be cramped.

It's also important to look for shoes with raised or walled toe boxes. Many of today's shoes have shallow, receding toe boxes. These cause problems for the toes because they lack adequate height in the shoe.

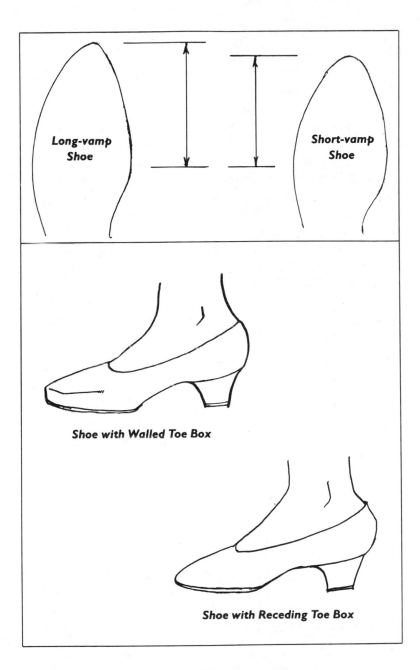

Long-vamp
Shoe

Short-vamp
Shoe

Shoe with Walled Toe Box

Shoe with Receding Toe Box

As long as your toes have freedom to move, you should have few problems with your feet. Many people have grown accustomed to wearing shoes that are too small for them. Don't let this happen to you!

The Shape of Your Foot Should Match the Shape of Your Shoes. I'm sure you've noticed all the tapered-toe shoes being shown today. I'd like you to take any pair of fashionable shoes you own, turn them upside down, and compare the shape of the front of the shoe to the shape of your foot. If you're like most people, your toes won't form the same neat, symmetrical pointed pattern that the shoe does. Most people's big toe is their longest, but many people's second or third toe is longest. Some of you have toes that form a squared-off pattern. I'm amazed at the number of women whose toes aren't symmetrically shaped wearing tapered-toe shoes. Needless to say, shoes like these are the

The Difference between Our Feet and Most Tapered-Toe Shoes

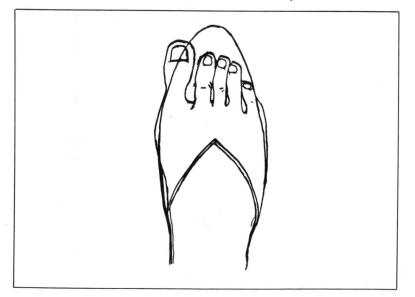

worst things for your feet. They press the toes together and keep them from functioning properly when you walk.

It's important not only to choose a shoe that's the right length and width for your foot, but also one that corresponds to your foot's shape. It's easy to tell if your shoes haven't been allowing your toes enough room. Look at your feet: Corns (either at the top, sides, or in between the toes), a heavy callus buildup, a bunion developing at the side of the big-toe joint, or toes beginning to take the shape of a tapered-toe shoe are all warning signals that your toes don't have enough space in your shoes.

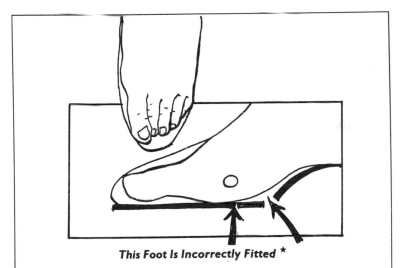

This Foot Is Incorrectly Fitted ★

These toes are cramped and twisted—stopping ventilation and creating excessive perspiration, which causes rotting of inner soles, linings, and upper leather. Short shoes like these cause enlarged big-toe joints and bunions, as well as general foot discomfort. Each step strains the foot arch. Without support under its entire arch span, the foot sags down. This causes nerves and blood vessels to become pinched, interfering with circulation. Trouble follows.

★*Courtesy of The Brannock Device Company, Syracuse, NY*

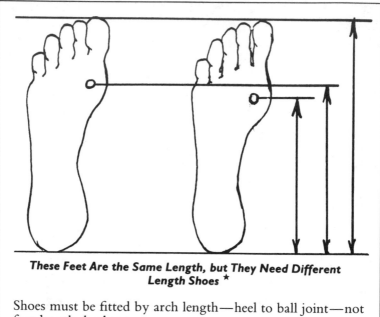

These Feet Are the Same Length, but They Need Different Length Shoes *

Shoes must be fitted by arch length—heel to ball joint—not foot length, heel to toe.

There are lasts for short-toed feet and lasts for long-toed feet. The correct last for a foot is one that accommodates the ball joint in its proper place and leaves enough space ahead of the toes, so they are not cramped or twisted.

*Courtesy of The Brannock Device Company, Syracuse, NY

Fit the Widest Part of Your Foot to the Widest Part of the Shoe. If I had to give you just one tip for fitting your feet comfortably, this would be it: Take a shoe in your hand and flex it as if you were walking. Notice that it bends at the widest part of the shoe. Coincidentally, when you walk your foot also flexes at its widest part, the ball of the foot. Doesn't it make sense, then, to fit the widest part of your foot to the widest part of the shoe?

People who ignore this are fitting their feet short by crowding the widest part of their foot toward the tapered end of a shoe. It may not always be possible to perfectly fit the widest part of your foot at the widest part of the shoe, but if you consciously aim for this every time you buy a pair of shoes, I guarantee you will be much more comfortable.

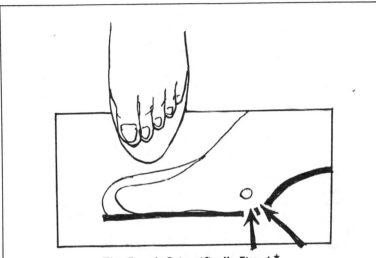

This Foot Is Scientifically Fitted *

When you accomplish this, you're assured of the most comfortable fit you can receive in that pair of shoes. The reasons for this are: The arch base of the shoe and the ball joint of the foot meet at the same point. The foot arch rests comfortably on the shank of the shoe, full length. The foot and the shoe bend at the same place—no sagging or gapping. Toes, too, are straight. There is ample space in front of them—no crowding, and plenty of ventilation. These feet will be comfortable, and these shoes will keep their shape.

Courtesy of The Brannock Device Company, Syracuse, NY

Why Do We Misfit Our Feet?

The biggest obstacle to properly fitted shoes is our over-emphasis on having them fit so snugly at the heel. Many women fit their feet tightly into a shoe just so they don't slip or gap at the heel. But their toes have no room to move.

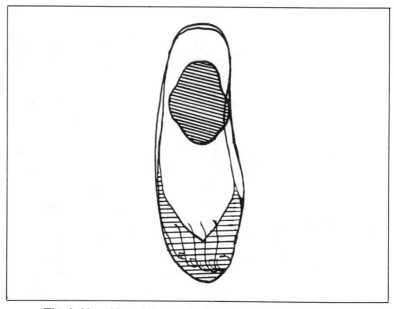

This Is How Many Women Fit Their Feet in Fashion Shoes

This illustration is typical of how many women fit their feet. Notice that the widest part of the foot is resting at a narrower part of the shoe than it should be. Here, comfort and freedom for the toes have been sacrificed for the sake of fitting the heel.

So what would happen if you were to go to a longer size? Your toes would have more room but the shoe would fit less tightly at the heel because the foot isn't stuffed into the shoe.

Unfortunately, fitting most pumps features this trade-off. More space for the toes in exchange for less fit in the heel, and vice versa. It's almost a no-win situation. For the health of your feet, I'd choose a bit less fit at the heel for more freedom of the toes. The risk of getting a blister at the heel is nothing compared to the consequences of a bunion.

How to Fit the Narrow Heel

Contrary to popular belief, slipping at the heel of a shoe does not occur because your heel bone is narrower than the rest of your foot. This is obvious and the shoe industry takes this into consideration when they craft a shoe by making the heel counter as narrow as possible so it will grip your heel snugly.

The heel counter of a shoe, no matter how narrow, cannot by itself hold the heel of a 120-pound woman wearing a shoe with a 2- or 3-inch heel and keep her foot from sliding away from the heel. The force of gravity is too powerful.

Slipping at the heel really starts at the other end of the shoe, at the ball of the foot. Here, feet are allowed to slide forward because of shoes that are too wide, too low-cut, or too high-heeled. To keep the foot from sliding forward and slipping at the heel, the shoe must exert just enough pressure at the ball, instep, or waist to hold the foot back in the shoe and push it against the heel.

How to Fit Both Your Toes *and* Heel Comfortably! The following styles will allow your toes freedom while fitting your heel because they keep the foot from sliding forward by holding a part of the foot other than the toes.

Oxfords. The most comfortable style you can wear. Its adjustable lacing holds the foot at the instep, allowing the toes freedom.

Strap shoes. Shoes with wide straps that hold the foot at the ankle or instep are excellent for support while holding the foot back against the heel.

Slingbacks. This style is good because each strap can be individually adjusted to fit each foot.

Boots. One of the best because there is so much "shoe" supporting the foot.

High-cut pumps. The higher the throat the better. Low-cut pumps allow the foot to slide forward in the shoe and away from the heel. If you can see the cleavage of your toes in your shoes, they are probably being cramped to keep the shoe on at the heel.

Low-heeled shoes. Feet slide forward much less in shoes with lower heels than those with high heels.

OTHER TIPS TO FIT THE NARROW HEEL

- Preflex the sole of your new shoes a couple of times after buying them and before wearing them. A stiff sole is harder to bend when walking, which makes it easier for the foot to lift out of the shoe at the heel.
- Watch out for unlined shoes and shoes made of extremely stretchable materials like suede. As soon as the shoe stretches at the ball, the foot slides forward and away from the heel.
- Don't let the salesperson go through the customary motion of "breaking in" the heel counter of the shoe with the palm of his hand. This can widen the heel counter too much.
- Avoid shoes with open sides.

A CHECKLIST TO FIT YOUR FEET BY

The following checkpoints must be considered *every* time you contemplate purchasing a pair of shoes.

Before trying on new shoes, check to see that the seams at the toes of your hosiery are on straight and that your hose aren't so tight that they confine your toes.

- Have your feet measured first. It's always a good idea to have *both* your feet measured, if for no other reason than they may periodically change size. Always have this done *while standing*, since your feet expand more when your full weight is on them.
- What condition are your feet in? Shop for shoes around midafternoon when your feet are neither at their smallest nor at their largest. Also, never shop for shoes when your feet hurt.
- Fit your larger (wider and/or longer) foot first. The shoe for the smaller foot should then be padded to take up any additional space and keep it from slipping at the heel.
- Always try on both shoes. Because most of our feet are slightly different from each other, you *must* try on *both* the right and left shoes every time you try on a new pair.
- If you have any doubts about fit, try the next size. The difference in length between a half size (6 to 6½) is only ⅙ *of an inch*, which isn't much. Don't buy shoes by *size*. Buy them by *fit*.
- Walk, walk, and walk some more in your new shoes before deciding to buy or keep them. You must test new shoes, whether at home or in the store, by walking in them *just as you would if you were walking outside*. Do this for at least **five minutes** before deciding on them.
- As a general rule, the narrower your foot, the higher the throat you can comfortably wear. A fleshier foot demands a shoe with a low-cut throat.

It's Not Easy Fitting Feet That Are Different Sizes and Constantly Change

The dilemma of properly fitting the feet is made even more difficult by the fact that even though our feet appear to be a mated pair, studies have shown that they are not. They may vary in the length of the toes, height of the arch, height of the instep, or width.

As if this wasn't bad enough, our feet take on many different sizes and shapes depending upon our activities, health, weather conditions, and the time of day. When standing, the foot widens and lengthens because its shock absorbers (the arches) partially collapse from our weight. When walking, this causes the foot to lengthen, backwards as well as forwards. Our feet also enlarge in hot or humid weather and become smaller when it's cold.

Check the Fit at...

The arch. When most people talk about their arches, they're referring to the inner longitudinal arch and the outer longitudinal arch. The inner arch functions as a spring, partially collapsing to absorb the shock of each step. This arch receives very little if any support from the shoe. A good-fitting shoe might cling to the under side of your inner arch, but it doesn't actually support it.

The outer arch should rest on the shank area of the shoe. Recheck the ball of your foot for proper placement so your foot will be in the best position to be supported by the arch. If your shoes have a large wrinkle behind the ball of the foot close to the inner, under side of the arch, this indicates that the ball is too far forward in the shoe.

If you have a high arch you may face some special problems. Much of your body's weight will be supported by the

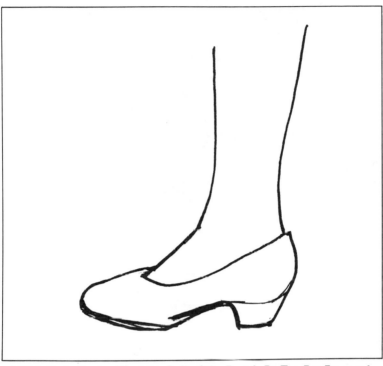

A Wrinkle Indicates That the Ball of the Foot Is Fit Too Far Forward in the Shoe

balls of your feet; therefore, it might be a good idea to add some padding to your shoes to absorb some of the shock. Adding a rubber half-sole to the bottom of your high-heel shoes or putting a cushioned insole (one that won't mat down) inside your shoes, under the balls of the feet, gives them needed shock absorbency.

The ball of the foot. You must have space at the ball of your foot so the foot can expand when you place your weight on it and as your foot swells throughout the day. To ensure this, you should be able to pinch a small amount of excess leather at the ball between your fingers.

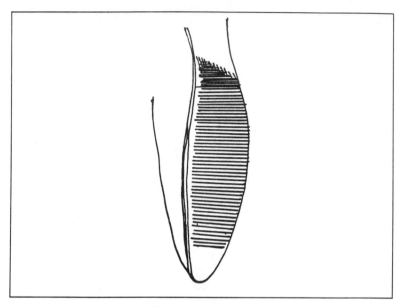

Rubber Half-Sole

If you have a bunion or any other joint problem, beware of shoes whose throat edge ends and cuts across the ball of the foot and sandal straps that don't fully cover this joint, as these cannot be stretched and will only cause you long-term pain. Look for shoes made of soft, pliable leathers that are cut up high enough to *cover* this area. Also, a shoe salesman or repairman can create a small pocket for this sensitive part of the foot by spot stretching it *before* you wear the shoes. Why break in a shoe if you don't have to?

The outer ball of the foot (joint at the base of the little toe). This is one of the most overlooked areas when fitting the foot and the reason why so many women have corns on the outside of their little toes. Just as the inner ball of the foot (the big toe joint) must meet the widest part of the shoe, so should the outer ball be fitted to the shoe at its widest part.

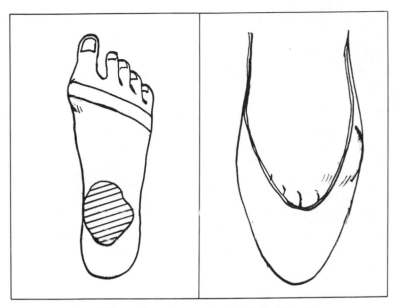

Avoid Shoes That Cut across the Ball of the Foot

The back of the heel. Some shoes will bite into your heel tendon or uncomfortably rub your heel bone. A shoe that feels tight here could be one that is really too tight *at the throat.* A tight throat forces the foot against the back of the shoe. If this happens to you, look for a style with a low or V-cut throat; try on a longer or wider shoe; or have the throat crimped by a repairman. All of these will allow your foot to settle into the shoe and move slightly away from the heel. You can also insert a heel pad under the lining, which will lift your foot above that part of the shoe that's irritating you.

The instep. If you have a high instep, you could have a problem with certain pumps, espadrilles, or other styles that come high up on the instep. U-cut or straight-across throats will probably cut into and bind the fleshy part of your foot.

Try wearing a low-cut vamp shoe to give your instep more room.

If you wear lace-up shoes and have a fleshy foot or high instep, try a blucher-style oxford. These easily accommo-

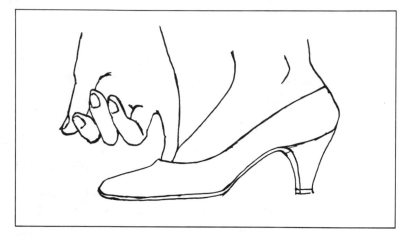

Make Sure You Can Fit a Part of Your Little Finger under the Throat Edge to Avoid Problems

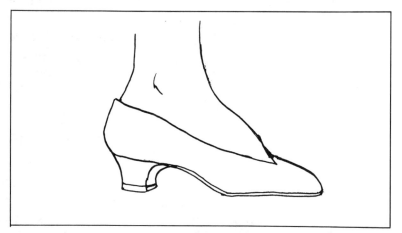

V-cut Vamp Shoes **Will Accommodate a High or Fleshy Instep**

date this type of foot. Avoid ghillies (a lace-up shoe without a tongue) because the shoelaces can easily dig into your instep.

Slip-on shoes or those with an elastic piece at the throat

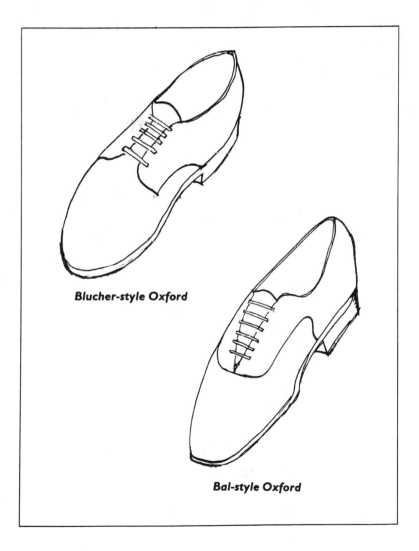

Blucher-style Oxford

Bal-style Oxford

can also bind the instep. If the shoe has elastic here, you can release it by using a pin to prick several holes in it. Be cautious of loafers that are cut high on the instep.

If your instep feels constrained by a boot, don't buy it. This part of the boot will rarely stretch on its own and will only cut into your foot every time you take a step.

If you have a narrow foot with a shallow instep, bal-style oxfords hold the foot more securely and prevent slippage at the heel.

The sides of the foot. The topline of the shoe should ideally fit snugly against your foot without cutting into the sides, the ankle, or any other protruding bones.

If your anklebone or the side of your foot is being cut by the topline, have a heel pad inserted underneath your heel.

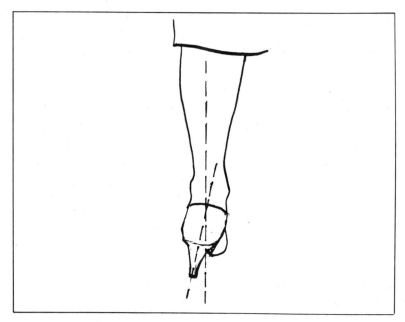

Pronated Foot

This lifts the foot above where it was being irritated. The edge of the topline can also be bent outward. If the topline has a sharp edge that cuts your foot, it can be filed down with an emery board.

If your foot pronates (turns inward), you'll benefit from a shoe with a lower cut topline, as your foot has more of a tendency to lean into and be cut by the shoe's inner topline.

The waist. This part of the foot lies between the instep and the ball. It's easy to tell if your foot has been fit too tightly here. Remove your shoes at the end of the day and look for a line on the top of your foot that corresponds to the throat of the shoe. If you see this, your foot wasn't given enough space here. It's extremely important to allow your foot extra space at the waist because of anticipated swelling. A shoe fit too tightly here can impede circulation, cause tingling or numbness in the toes, and additional swelling, as well as irritation where the shoe cuts into the foot. NOTE: Make sure the shoe has enough room for you to slip the end of your little finger under the throat edge.

"Is It Possible My Feet Are Still Growing?" Have you noticed that your feet don't quite fit into some of your old shoes as comfortably as they once did? Do some shoes seem more confining than before? If so, here are a few things you should be aware of.

- Feet change with age. The wear and tear we subject our feet to over a lifetime eventually takes its toll. Constant pounding on hard surfaces in high-fashion shoes eventually causes the arch to collapse slightly over time. As this happens the foot lengthens.
- Your feet may be retaining more fluid than normal. If this appears to be the case, check with your physician, as it may signal a problem elsewhere in your body.

- If you're pregnant or you've just had a baby, expect your feet to grow by half a shoe size. When a woman has a baby, the body prepares for delivery by loosening the ligaments. With the extra weight of the expectant mother, the feet, in most cases, will spread and grow in size.
- Wearing pointed-toe shoes may require you to go one-half size longer to accommodate your toes, particularly if you have wide feet.

Feet do not grow after the ages of 18 to 21, yet the above reasons may help to explain why your feet appear to still be growing.

The Most Common Shoe-Fitting Problems

Burning on the Balls of the Feet. The following are some of the reasons why you may experience burning on the balls of your feet.

Wearing high heels. The higher the heel, the more your body's weight is centered on the balls of the feet rather than being evenly supported by the entire foot. This not only causes excessive callus buildup but also results in your feet being sorer than they should be at the end of the day.

Callus buildup on the balls of your feet causes burning because this thickened tissue has lost its elasticity and does not bend or stretch when the foot bends like normal tissue does. This thicker skin also doesn't breathe, which produces a burning, sticking sensation when walking.

Man-made soles tend to build up heat within the shoe, which is then transmitted through the sole to your feet. Rubber and crepe soles also build up heat by catching on rugs and sidewalks, causing the shoe to stop while the foot slides forward in them. After continually sliding back and forth, the soles of the feet begin to burn from constant friction.

Also, check your hosiery. If they're too tight around your toes, they won't be allowed to extend forward and spread, which concentrates the body's weight on the balls of the feet.

One thing you can do is add some cushioning to your shoes. I recommend Spenco, a nitrogen-impregnated foam-rubberlike substance that is extremely shock absorbent and outlasts ordinary foam rubber.

WHY YOU WON'T ALWAYS WEAR THE SAME SIZE IN EVERY SHOE

- The shoe industry has no standard measurements for size. They have guidelines, but no one is required to follow them.
- Heel height. Because the foot moves around more (forwards and backwards) in a low-heel shoe, you may wear a half-size longer in this type of shoe.
- Sizes differ from style to style. You may wear a shorter size in a round or square-toe shoe than in a tapered-toe style. Also, different types of shoes (loafers, boots, pumps, and oxfords) all fit differently.
- Unlined shoes stretch more than lined shoes. These often have to be bought slightly tighter because of how much they stretch.
- Different materials have different fit characteristics. Normally softer, more pliable materials (such as suede) can be fit more snuggly than other nongiving materials, such as manmades and many reptile skins. These have to be bought with a perfect fit since they give very little with wear.
- Some shoes require different hose than others. If you intend to wear shoes with heavy socks, you will probably need a larger size. (Remember to try on the shoes with the appropriate hose.)

PROS AND CONS OF HIGH HEELS

Studies have linked high heels with problems of the feet as well as with other parts of the body. High heels shift the body's weight forward, putting stress on the skeleton (especially the knees and lower back). This unnatural position forces the muscles to work harder to keep the body upright.

Flats, on the other hand, are not the answer either. Calf ache is a very common problem for women who often wear flat or very low heels. They can also cause knee pain, especially if you have shortened calf muscles or Achilles tendinitis.

The optimum heel height is 1½", which evenly distributes the body's weight between the ball of the foot, the heel, and the arch.

Tips for wearing high heels

- They should not be worn all day, every day. Calf muscles may become shortened and lower back trouble can result from wearing high heels constantly.
- Alternate the height of your heels throughout the week. But don't go from very high heels to flats all at once. Your heel cord can't take this radical change and your feet and/or legs may ache as a result.
- High-heel shoes with thick heels are better than those with thin heels.

Gapping at the Topline of the Shoe. Let's look at the difference between a shoe that gaps and one that opens up as part of the natural heel-to-toe flexing that occurs when you walk. Take one of your pumps and hold it at the back of the heel. Put it on a table and lift the heel as you would when walking. Notice how the sides of the shoe open up. Problem gapping occurs when the shoe is not flexed and it still gaps.

Here are some reasons why shoes gap and how to avoid it.

If your feet pronate (turn in), the inner sides of your feet will hit the inner topline of the shoe and cause it to pooch out or gap. This happens less in shoes with heels over 2″ high. Adding a heel pad to your lower-heel shoes will help lessen gaping.

Styles that are cut low at the topline easily gap. You can avoid this by looking for shoes whose topline is not scooped too low.

Styles that have little or no heel counter gap easily. Unconstructed styles, such as moccasins and loafers, gap much more than constructed styles because they have little or no heel counter and often no lining.

Gapping occurs **more in shoes that** properly *fit the ball of the foot* than in those that do not. Remember the low-vamp shoe that we had to pack the foot into to keep it on the heel? (See page 38.) Even though this shoe did not fit correctly, the pressure the foot exerted into the front and back of the shoe kept the topline of the shoe taut and no gapping occurred. Whereas a foot correctly fit from ball to heel, which allows the toes room to move, is not pushing into the end of the shoe and some gapping will occur.

Gapping can also be caused by an extra-wide or fleshy heel that opens the shoe up at the heel counter.

Although the appearance of a shoe that gaps is disturbing, it is usually the look and not the feel of the shoe that bothers women most. In fact, with our imperfect feet, and tapered-toe shoes, some gapping is expected.

"I Can't Keep a Slingback on My Heel." Many women believe they cannot wear a slingback shoe. Yet, in ten years of selling shoes, the *only* women I have seen who genuinely cannot wear them are those whose heel bone has little or no indentation for a strap to hang upon.

The most common complaint I hear about slingback shoes is that the strap won't stay on the heel. The reason these straps fall off is because the shoe eventually stretches and the foot slides forward and away from the strap. Although the strap can be tightened, this only forces the foot into the narrowing toe box. What you should do is have the shoe padded (under the ball of the foot), which will restore it back to its original width. This keeps the foot from sliding forward and pushes the ball of the foot back into the widest part of the shoe and the heel back against the sling strap.

"My Toes Are Being Cut by the Edge of an Open-toe Shoe." This happens because many shoe manufacturers cut open-toe shoes a half-size shorter than they are marked so there won't be as much extra space beyond the end of your toes. Then, when you walk, your toes—which are already too close to the front of the shoe—jut into the edge of the toe opening.

Your first inclination might be to have the shoes stretched. Instead, double-check the placement of the balls of your feet to make sure they meet the widest part of the shoe. Going to a longer length to accommodate the ball of the foot will move your toes back in the shoe, away from the toe opening just enough to allow for forward extension of the toes.

How to Fit the Flexible Foot. A flexible foot is one whose arch stretches an abnormal amount with weight-bearing. This foot is very difficult to fit because it moves around so much inside the shoe and it needs a lot of support. The best shoe for this type of foot is one that comes up high on the waist/instep or has straps to hold the foot at the ankle or across the instep.

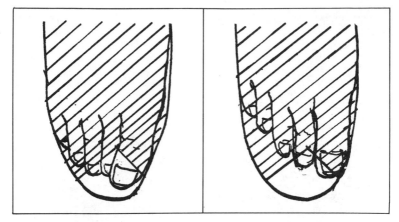

**These Toes Are Too Close to
the End of the Shoe**

**Where Your Toes Should Be
Fit in an Open-toe Shoe**

Fitting Orthotics in Fashion Shoes. Many women now
wear orthotics in their shoes. Often erroneously referred to
as arch supports, these orthotics are usually prescribed by
podiatrists or chiropodists to correct inherited structural im-
balances.

When fitted into the right type of shoe, they work quite
well; however, extra allowance must be made to accommodate both the foot and the orthotic. An orthotic placed into a
regular shoe often causes the foot to slip at the heel and is
tight at the ball of the foot. This happens because it lifts the
foot up and sometimes out of the shoe as well as taking up
additional space.

If you must wear an orthotic, you'll probably need to buy
your shoes one width wider than normal. Styles that open
up at the instep such as oxfords and athletic shoes accommodate the foot better than most other shoes. Boots are also
good. Styles that cannot be worn with orthotics are open
shoes such as sandals, slingbacks, and low-cut pumps.

Common Misconceptions about Fitting the Feet and Buying Shoes

"Padding a Shoe Never Works. If a Shoe Needs Any Adjustment, Then It Isn't for Me."

What exactly do you mean by padding? Padding means putting a filler inside a shoe (usually underneath the ball of the foot) to keep one foot (sometimes both) from slipping at the heel by pushing the foot back into the heel.

Although to some of you padding a shoe may seem like a desperate salesperson's attempt to sell a shoe, padding really *does* work. It wouldn't be needed if our feet were exactly the same, but this is rarely the case. Most of us have feet that are different enough to require that some kind of filler be put in our shoes (especially pumps) to make them fit each foot in the same way. I look at padding as custom fitting each foot.

When does a shoe need to be padded? If your feet (or one foot) need an in-between size, say an A width, yet you can only find B and AA width shoes, what do you do? Buy the shoe in the wider B width and have them padded to make them the required A width.

Another benefit of having your shoes padded is the additional cushioning your feet receive, which helps buffer them from the impact shock of walking on hard pavements.

Doesn't padding a shoe make it too tight? Not if it's done correctly, using the proper material (cork, felt, and foam are all used). All a pad does is take up additional space in the shoe where you can afford it most (at the widest part of the shoe) to keep your foot from sliding into the narrowing vamp of the shoe.

Where do you draw the line with pads? You shouldn't have three or four pads put in your shoes to make them fit. This is a major alteration and should be avoided.

"Will Heel Grips Really Keep My Heels from Slipping?" I don't care for heel grips. They keep the heel from slipping by pushing the foot forward until the toes hit the end of the shoe. The only time I would even consider using them is if the shoe had already been padded at the ball of the foot to keep it from sliding any farther forward.

TIPS FOR FITTING BOOTS

In addition to using the same checkpoints for fitting a pair of shoes, keep these tips in mind:

- Don't buy boots that bind the ankle or instep.
- Don't buy a boot that is too tight around the calf. Make sure you can fit one of your fingers inside the boot at the top of the calf to ensure your leg won't be constricted.
- Boots usually slip some at the heel when you first buy them (particularly low-heel boots). This improves with wear as the sole becomes more flexible and the heel counter breaks down from your foot's perspiration and begins to mold to your heel.
- If you have a narrow foot, don't settle for boots that aren't made in narrow widths. If you do, you may have to wear a couple of pairs of socks just to keep them on.
- If you have a tough time pulling on your boot, remember to grab and pull it at the back seam (at the Achilles tendon right behind your anklebone).
- Avoid wearing boots indoors all day long, especially foul-weather boots. Your feet will perspire more than normal as heat cannot easily escape from boots. This will not only be uncomfortable, but can also lead to bacterial infections.
- It's a good idea to put talcum or baby powder inside your boots before you wear them to help keep your feet dry. You can also use these powders when putting on a snug-fitting boot without a zipper, as they'll slide on more easily.

"If the Front Part of My Foot Feels Tight, I Need a Wider Width Shoe." If the front part of your foot feels tight, the first thing you should check is the placement of the ball of your foot. If it is too far forward in the shoe, it will feel tight. In this case, a *longer* shoe gives your feet more *width*. Many wider feet need a half-size longer shoe.

If the ball of your foot is at the widest part of the shoe and it still feels tight, then you do need a wider width shoe.

"Why Is It That Only a Few Manufacturers Make Shoes in Narrow or Wide Widths and Short or Long Sizes?" Manufacturers do make these sizes, but most shoe stores just don't carry them.

4
SHOE CARE, REPAIR, AND MAINTENANCE

With the high cost of shoes these days, it makes sense to take care of the shoes you own. The tips outlined below are designed to save you money by keeping your shoes looking nicer, performing better, and lasting longer.

Much of this chapter deals with shoes which have, at the very least, leather uppers. Leather shoes are more likely to be repaired, rather than thrown out, because they're easily fixed and expensive to replace.

NOTE: I will recommend many different shoe-care products. Make sure to read *all* of the instructions *very* carefully *before* you use any of them.

How to Protect Your Shoes

No question about it, a shoe that has been protected lasts longer, is easier to clean, wears better, and needs to be replaced less often. Pretreating your shoes is similar to putting a coat of wax on your car. Applying the right protectant to your shoes *before* you wear them keeps scuffs, dirt, and spilled liquids on the *surface* of the shoe, where they are easier to remove later on.

The type of protectant you use depends upon

- What you'll be using the shoes for.
- The climate and conditions you'll be wearing them in.
- The type of material the shoe is made of.

Leather lotion protects fine leathers best. It contains at least 90% lanolin and cannot harm leather no matter what the tannery has done to treat it chemically. A coat, spread over the entire upper of the shoes, *before they are worn,* serves as a buffer from scuffs, water, salt, dirt, and other things that get into and destroy leathers. Using a leather lotion periodically keeps leather uppers soft, flexible, and allows them to breathe. If you wear your shoes a couple of times a week, you should treat them with lotion at least once a month.

Use a silicone-based, water-repellent spray on leather shoes that are exposed to bad weather. It makes them spot-resistant and helps prevent stains by keeping liquids and dirt on the surface of the shoe, where they're easily cleaned. If you wear your shoes often in bad weather, you should reapply this spray every month or so.

CAUTION: Using too much of this spray can keep the upper from breathing. These are advertised to "keep water out while letting the leather breathe," but it seems to me that something which seals the pores from the outside would also keep them from breathing from the inside. Also, don't use sprays labeled "silicone spray" on light-colored leather or suede shoes. These contain heavier concentrations of silicone and can darken the upper.

Protecting Leather Boots in Bad Weather.

A good calfskin boot should be protected with *both* a liberal coat of leather lotion and a water repellent. These will keep the skin supple and prevent water and salt from penetrating into the leather. First, spray the boot with water repellent, apply the leather lotion, then buff with a cloth. This wears off in time, and if you constantly wear them in bad weather, this process should be repeated after every cleaning or once every few weeks.

Cowhide or split leather boots. Use mink oil on leathers such as these, which you're not too concerned about aesthetically. It has a natural fat residue that lubricates and softens the leather in addition to waterproofing it. Saddle soap conditions, cleans, preserves, and softens these leathers, but it does cake. Sno-Seal is a good protectant for heavier leathers but the application process is a bit more involved.

CAUTION: Don't use mink oil or saddle soap on supple leathers like kidskin, calfskin, or suede. Mink oil can also darken medium- to light-colored leathers and leave a greasy film that is difficult to remove.

Pretreating Other Upper Materials.

Fabric shoes. All fabric shoes (canvas, linen, rope, silk, satin) should be protected with either a Scotchguard Fabric Protector or a silicone-based water repellent. These are absorbed into the fibers of the fabric upper, keeping liquids, grease, and dirt on the surface. This enables you to blot off a spill before it enters the fabric, making it easier to remove spots later on. These protectants need to be reapplied every month or so, especially after a shoe has been cleaned.

Metallic finishes. Use leather lotion or Meltonian Delicate Cream.

Patent shoes. Whether they are real or synthetic, patent shoes need no pretreatment. To keep patent soft and pliable, use petroleum jelly. Should you scuff the shoe, the scuff will slide off, not marring the finish because you're only taking off the greasy residue. Apply before you wear the shoe, and rub it in with a soft cloth. It won't mar the finish and it leaves a nice shine.

Exotics. Alligator, crocodile, lizard, snakeskin, and ostrich don't really need to be pretreated, but you can use Meltonian Delicate Cream to keep the skins from drying out, cracking, or fraying. First test a small, inconspicuous area at the back of the shoe to make sure it doesn't dull the luster of the skin. Apply only a small amount and afterwards, rub off any excess cream with a soft cloth. With snakeskin, rub the cream in the direction of the scales.

Suedes. These should always be protected with a silicone-based water repellent.

Synthetics. These need no pretreatment.

Do Soles Need to Be Pretreated? Not unless you plan to wear a leather-soled shoe or boot in heavy snow or water. When wearing heavier leather boots for winter you may want to spray or daub some liquid silicone around the seams of the sole to keep water from seeping in.

What's the Difference between "Waterproof" and "Water Repellent"? To be water*proof* a shoe or boot must be made in one piece of either rubber, plastic, or vinyl. It cannot have seams, stitching, zippers, or a separate sole, because water can seep through these. Since waterproof shoes or boots are completely sealed to keep water out, they don't breathe to let air in and can be hot and clammy.

Water *repellent* has come to mean a finish applied to leather or fabric that resists or repels water. In the case of a shoe, the upper still breathes some, as the pores are not totally sealed. But, when immersed, water will eventually seep through this finish.

How to Take Care of Your Shoes between Wearings

Wipe Off Your Shoes before Putting Them Away. Use a horsehair brush on leather shoes and a plastic bristle brush on suede shoes to clean off any surface dirt. Do this before dirt is allowed to accummulate and becomes embedded in the pores of the upper.

Inspect Them after Each Wearing. Inspect your shoes for any spots. These are easier to remove while they are fresh rather than once they've been on the shoe for a while.

Additionally, look for the following problems before you put your shoes away.

- Heel lifts that are wearing down.
- Linings that are wearing thin or tearing.
- Scuffs that need attention.
- Gouged leather at the heel or toe.
- A sole that is separating from the upper.
- Thin, worn-out soles.
- Cracked, curled-up sock linings or those darkened from perspiration.
- Paddings that have matted down.
- Laces that are about to break.
- Tassels or other ornaments coming loose.

Small repairs attended to early never get the chance to become major repairs. At this stage, most shoes can easily be repaired and will in the long run cost you less money.

Allow Your Shoes to Air Out for *at Least* 24 Hours. It is extremely important to rest your shoes at least one, preferably two, days between wearings to allow them to dry and air out. Each of our feet perspires an average of ½ *cup* per day. Much of this perspiration is made up of salts and acids that eat away at leathers (especially the linings), causing them to crack and fray if allowed to accumulate. Also, a shoe that is constantly worn builds up moisture and becomes an incubator for bacterial growth. The following are tips to help save your shoes from, and lessen, foot perspiration.

- Use foot powder inside your shoes. It absorbs moisture.
- Use *cedar* shoe trees. For good leather shoes, it's the best investment you can make because they
  —absorb moisture from the linings of shoes,
  —keep wrinkles from setting into the upper,
  —keep the shoe from curling up,
  —keep the linings from cracking as the shoe dries in a taut form, and
  —make shoes easier to polish. Creases are smoothed out, which makes for a smoother polishing surface.

Cedar shoe trees should be kept inside your shoes for two days, then left out for a day to let moisture evaporate from the shoe tree. When their scent begins to fade, rub them lightly with fine sandpaper.

How Should You Store Boots? Cedar shoe trees should be used in boots, too. Plastic boot trees are excellent for keeping the shaft of the boot upright and preventing it from folding in half or wrinkling at the ankle. These come in different calf heights and should be placed in the boots when they're not being used. A piece of rolled up cardboard also works well.

CARING FOR SHOES AND BOOTS ONCE THEY'VE BEEN CAUGHT IN BAD WEATHER

- Take them off as soon as possible. Shoes can easily stretch out of shape if they are worn while wet.
- To avoid a water line from forming on the shoe, wet the entire shoe so it dries evenly.
- Wipe off as much water as you can with a clean, damp sponge.
- Stuff the shoes loosely with newspaper, paper towels, or face cloths until they are almost dry. Don't pack them tightly; they need room for air to circulate.
- Never dry wet shoes near a direct source of heat or light. No sun, heaters, or hair dryers! These cause leather to become brittle and crack as well as baking in the stains.
- Before the shoes are completely dry, put shoe trees or new toweling inside of them.
- After they've dried, condition smooth leathers with a lotion and then polish. Suede shoes should be steamed by holding them at a distance over a tea kettle and brushed with a terry-cloth towel to restore the nap.

Cleaning Your Shoes

Many upper materials require specialized cleaners, while most synthetic materials require nothing more than soap and water. While you could rub almost anything on a heavy man's shoe and not ruin them, you've got to be very careful when working with many fine leathers used in women's shoes because they're so delicate.

The best all-purpose cleaner for smooth leathers and synthetics is leather *lotion*. This lanolin-based lotion easily cleans surface dirt and light marks from most shoes. For tough dirt and pen marks try leather *balm*, which contains a detergent as well as softening and cleaning agents. CAUTION: Use sparingly on delicate leathers.

Using each of these requires putting a small amount on a *clean* cloth and rubbing it into the leather with a circular motion. Apply only to small areas of the shoe at a time, wiping off the dirt almost immediately while the cream is still moist. Use a *clean* part of the cloth for each part of the shoe. For really tough spots on heavier calfskins and cowhide-type leathers, use Lexol leather cleaner and conditioner, which works very well but involves a more complicated application. If you have any doubts about what you are doing, take your shoes to a skilled shoe repairman.

The following are suggested for cleaning specific upper materials.

Delicate leathers. Use Meltonian Delicate Cream.

Calfskin. Leather lotion is great for cleaning off dirt and minor scuffs; leather balm for minor stains and deeper scuffs.

Cowhide and split leather. Use leather balm or saddle soap. I prefer leather balm because it has more softening and cleaning agents than saddle soap. Saddle soap lifts grease and dirt from heavier leathers and conditions it, too.

Fabric shoes (canvas, linen, macrame, rope, peau de soie). Constructed (lined) evening shoes should be taken to a shoe repairman. There are too many things that can go wrong if you try to do them yourself.

Unconstructed shoes like canvas espadrilles, in which the upper is cemented to the sole, can be cleaned by using a bar of soap (not liquid detergent) sparingly, water, and a sponge or nailbrush.

Here's how:

- Stuff both shoes with a face cloth or toweling.

- Holding them upside down so the water drips away from the sole, scrub only the upper lightly, being careful not to wet the seams, trim, or stitching, as they might bleed.
- Still holding the shoes upside down, rinse them off with a nailbrush as often as you need to remove the soapy residue. Restuff the shoes with dry toweling and let them dry away from any direct source of heat.
- After they have dried, reapply a water repellent.

Man-made materials. These can be cleaned with almost anything. Patent-leather cleaners, household glass cleaners, soap and water, leather-vinyl cleaners, and leather lotions all work fine. Try using a damp cloth first. CAUTION: Avoid using cleaners that contain solvents.

Patent leather. Be it real or synthetic, patent can be cleaned and polished with a glass cleaner, leather lotion, a damp cloth, petroleum jelly, or any one of many patent-leather cleaners. CAUTION: Be careful of cleaners that have an alcohol base. The alcohol may dry out real patent leather, causing it to crack and peel.

Reptile leathers. Use a foam reptile cleaner for all exotic leathers.

For snakeskin, take a clean, damp cloth and using either water, leather lotion, or delicate cream, wipe the skin in the direction of the scales, making sure not to rub against the grain. Never polish snakeskin; it can ruin the finish. Over time snakeskin can lose its luster and look dull. Some repairmen can reglaze these shoes to bring back the original shiny finish.

For crocodile and alligator, use a horsehair brush between wearings to remove dirt between the scales and seams. Both leather lotion and Meltonian Delicate Cream can be used to clean and moisture these skins. CAUTION: Some creams and lotions can dull the finish of these skins.

ADVICE FOR REMOVING TOUGH SPOTS

- The spot or stain has to be fresh. If something has had a chance to settle into the shoe surface, it may be impossible to remove later on.
- Don't clean light suede shoes, or difficult stains such as oil, ink, or tar yourself. Take them to a professional.
- Don't attempt to dry-clean shoes yourself.
- Be cautious of spot cleaning. It is very easy to overwork an area, worsen it, and create another spot. It's best to go over the *entire* shoe.

    NOTE: If you don't know what you are doing or the stain looks tough, don't even try to clean it yourself. Take it to an expert.

Suede. A good bristle brush should be used to get into the pores of the nap and keep dust and dirt from settling in. Any stains should be attended to as soon as possible to prevent them from becoming permanent.

To raise the nap of suede that has matted down, and to remove scratches, scuffs, and light stains, use very fine sandpaper or an emery board. Rub the suede lightly and then brush out any leftover particles. An art gum eraser and a Suede Stone also work well.

Caked-on dirt can be removed by holding the shoe at a distance over a steaming tea kettle while brushing it to raise the nap again. This also works well with suede that has hardened up.

If your suede shoes have become badly faded over time, there are products that can restore their original color (the darker the shoe, the more effective).

CAUTION: Suede is one of the most difficult materials to clean correctly. Some cleaners can cause the color of the shoe to lighten. Check for colorfastness by applying a small amount to an inconspicuous area near the heel. If any of the color rubs off, discontinue use.

White leather. These summer shoes are almost impossible to clean well. Even good shoe repairmen find that refinishing is more effective than cleaning once this leather has been scuffed.

To clean surface dirt and minor scuffs from white leather, use a leather lotion, soap and water, or a cleaner made especially for white-leather shoes.

Most white polishes only temporarily cover scuffs while white refinishing products that come in aerosol containers (like a spray dye) do a good job restoring some of the color. Cadillac White Refinish and Meltonian White Polish are also excellent products for white shoes.

Miscellaneous leathers. Bright-colored shoes can be cleaned with a leather lotion or Meltonian Delicate Cream. To cover scuff marks that won't come off, try using a cream polish of the same color.

Metallic leathers can be cleaned by putting a *small* amount of window cleaner or leather lotion *on a cloth* and then going over the specific area *lightly* to remove scuffs and dirt. A shoe that is badly scuffed or peeling can be partially refinished at that area by a repairman. Refinishing the entire shoe changes the original color.

Matte (dull) finish leathers can have some marks erased by rubbing an art gum eraser lightly over the mark. Really tough spots should be taken to a repairman.

How to Cope with Salt Stains. If you have protected your shoes or boots *prior* to wearing them in snow, salt-stain removers are pretty effective. It's when nothing has been applied to them beforehand that these hard-to-remove stains become embedded in the leather.

The first thing you should do is wipe off any dirt and salt with a soft brush. Next, dab the *entire* boot or shoe (heels and soles, too) with a solution of 1 part white vinegar to 3 parts water. If this isn't done immediately, the salt will eat away at the leather. Next, using a clean sponge, rinse with clear water and let the shoes dry as instructed on page 65. Finally, condition with a leather lotion and then polish. For cowhide-type leathers, rub on a light coat of saddle soap, making sure *not* to create a lather. Next, wipe off the excess and let the shoes dry again. After they dry, use a good cream polish.

If you can't clean salt stains off right away, seal your boots or shoes in a plastic bag so they'll stay moist until you can get to them.

Polishing and Shining Your Shoes

Even though today's leather shoes are dyed with top quality dyes and finishes, it's no wonder that the color fades quickly considering what we subject them to. Therefore, to keep your shoes looking new, it's important to polish them periodically. In addition to restoring color to the shoe, a good polish also moisturizes and conditions the leather to keep it from drying out and looking worn.

Before Polishing Your Shoes... brush off any surface dirt and then clean them. It's important to have all the right tools for the job. Here is what you'll need to do it right:

- A small, round applicator brush with a handle to apply the polish with, although a soft cloth will do.
- A horsehair brush for removing excess polish.
- An old toothbrush.
- A soft cotton or lamb's-wool cloth.

Choosing the Right Polish. First, match the polish as closely as possible to the color of the leather. Most shoe repair shops carry an extensive array of colors. If you can't find the right one, use a *lighter* shade, or a neutral cream.

CAUTION: It's very easy to darken a shoe if you're not careful. If you are not sure, test some on a small, inconspicuous spot at the back of the heel. Certain leathers should not be polished. Dull, unfinished natural leathers and delicate leathers should not be polished, as they may darken and become permanently stained.

Liquid Polish, Cream Polish, or Paste Wax?

Liquids are good for scuffs, though they cover rather than remove them. Most liquid polishes contain wax and lanolin, which condition leathers and keep them soft and supple. But they can leave a waxy buildup on the shoe that should be completely cleaned off every once in a while.

Creams are the most commonly used polishes for good leather shoes. They contain lanolin and dyes to revitalize the color. They clean and soften leathers well, since they are rubbed in by hand in contrast to liquid polishes, which are applied to the surface.

Paste waxes are also a surface polish. They're used almost exclusively on men's shoes, since they give a very high gloss finish. Waxes do a great job of repelling rain and snow, but tend to build up over time and can chip and crack where the shoe flexes. Another drawback to using a wax polish is that they don't nourish the leather. They provide a high sheen but at the same time close off the pores, which let the shoe breathe. This can lead to the upper cracking, peeling, and rotting, as well as increasing foot perspiration. CAUTION: Do not use wax on fine, delicate leathers because it is absorbed into the shoe and can stain it.

How to Give Your Shoes a Professional Polish.

- If you have shoe trees, leave them in the shoes while polishing to smooth out creases and wrinkles.

- Using a round brush, or a cloth, apply a small amount of polish to the shoe with a circular motion, beginning at the toe and working back toward the heel. Use a toothbrush to remove any polish you've gotten into the seams or perforations.

- Let each shoe dry for about five minutes.

- Take a horsehair brush and buff the shoe *lightly* to remove any excess polish.

- Buff the shoe with the polishing cloth, doing one area at a time, until you get a nice shine.

CAUTION: Be careful when brushing fine, soft leathers (especially light colors). Friction caused by brushing the leather back and forth could cause scratches and mar the finish. If you're unsure, use a soft cloth.

When polishing a shoe, don't rub too hard or too frequently. You can burn the leather with friction and take some of the finish off. A light-colored leather can develop a dark spot and a dark leather may blemish.

What about Those Quick-Sponge Polishes? Beware of using quick-wipe, self-shine products on fine leathers. Their alcohol base will seal up the leather and dry it out. These polishes, at best, give only a temporary sheen that fades quickly. Instant-shine polishes are nothing more than silicone on a sponge. All they do is wipe off the excess dirt and put a luster on the shoe. Silicone won't really harm the shoe, but it does close off the pores somewhat. All you get is a high shine because of the glaze on top.

Minor Repairs You Can Do Yourself

Fixing Nicks and Cuts on Your Shoes. If the heel or toe of your shoe has been nicked and there's still a piece of leather hanging from it, glue down the remaining piece with *rubber cement*. Let it dry, then polish.

If there isn't enough leather left to glue down, use an emery board to smooth down the surface and then a felt-tip pen, shoe polish, or a crayon to recolor the bare spot. This works best with dark leathers.

Punching Holes in Straps. If you don't have access to a hole punch, use a hammer and a small nail. First, press the nail lightly where you'd like the new hole. Remove it for a second to make sure you have the right spot, and then give it a good whack with the hammer.

Filing Down Thread Knots. If there's something inside your shoe that's tearing your hosiery, it's probably just an unfinished thread knot. Run your hand along the edges and insides of the shoe until you feel the knot. Then, using an emery board, file it down until smooth.

Loose Threads. Loose strands of thread can easily be eliminated by taking a match to them (for a second or two), which will melt them down to a little knot. The remaining knot can then be filed down with an emery board for a smooth finish.

Give Your Toes More Space by Lifting the Toe Box. Holding the front of the shoe, gently insert a broomstick handle into the toe box and give it a few twists while continuing to push the broom handle into the end of the shoe. You may get a slight separation of the upper from the sole at the toe area, so don't overdo it.

Scuff Up the Soles of Your Shoes so They Don't Slip.
There are a number of different ways you can rough up the
soles of new shoes so you won't slip when first wearing
them.

- Rub them with a file or sandpaper.
- Walk carefully to a sidewalk and do "the twist."
- Purchase an adhesive sandpaperlike covered pad that
  sticks to the soles of your shoes and gives them added
  traction.

Stretch Your Own Shoes. Right before you are about to
wear a pair of new shoes, put some Magix Shoe Stretch on
your fingers and dab it along the insides of your shoes—
especially along the sides of the toes. This allows the leather
to soften and mold to your foot more quickly than if you
were to try and break in the shoes on your own.

When Should You Take Your Shoes to a Repair Shop?

- While the problem is still small.
- If the cost of the repair is less than the price of a new
  pair of shoes. If your favorite shoes are irreplaceable,
  then price is no object.
- A shoe can be repaired as long as the upper is in good
  shape. Good leather shoes can be repaired over and
  over. It's not worth repairing a shoe, however, if the
  lining has cracked through to the upper, if the lining has
  blackened from sweating, or if the upper has stretched
  totally out of shape.

Repairs Most Shops Are Capable of Doing

You'd be amazed at what a good shoe repairman can do for your shoes. Below are listed some of the more common repairs.

Heel Repairs.

Replacing heel lifts. The heels of your shoes support about 25% of your body weight and absorb much of the shock your body receives when you walk. When heel lifts wear down, it puts uneven pressure on your heel bone and the rest of your body as it strains to balance itself. Heel lifts should be replaced when they've worn down about halfway. Never let them wear down so far that they're entirely worn off because part of the heel can become ruined, too. If this happens, both heels have to be shortened to matching heights before a new lift can be added.

These days, most heeled shoes use nylon or polyurethane lifts instead of rubber or leather because these don't wear as long. Unfortunately, nylon and polyurethane can skid and slip on pavements. Ask your repairman to give your shoes the best lift he has that combines shock absorbency, durability, and skid resistance.

Raising or lowering the height of a heel. Shoe repairmen can raise or lower the height of a heel from ⅛" to ¼" without measurably altering the balance of the shoe. How much can be done depends upon the shoe.

Changing the heel. Some shoe-repair shops carry an extensive stock of different shape heels, enabling you to change those heels that are dated.

Re-covering the heel. One of the biggest complaints women have are the scrapes and gouges their heels receive from city streets, chairs, and the pedals of their cars. A repairman can take an unsightly heel and re-cover it with a new piece of leather or stacked leather veneer, or stretch out the remaining leather, cement down the loose ends, and then touch up the heel with a color close to the original.

Also, there are products you can buy to take care of this problem. Some protect the heel by covering it with a sleeve of plastic, while another, much like fingernail polish, paints over scuffs and scrapes in a matching color.

Laces. Have you ever had the tip of your shoelaces come off and then tried to thread the lace through an eyelet? Shoe repairmen can put a new tip on laces like these.

Padding a Shoe. A shoe repairman can pad your shoes so they don't slip in the heel or add arch supports, metatarsal pads, cushioned insoles, and other pads to your shoes.

Relasting (Narrowing) Shoes. Shoe repairmen can also make a shoe narrower. They do this by opening up the sole of the shoe and then tightening the lasting margin underneath it.

Resoling a Shoe. When the soles of your shoes begin wearing thin, don't wait for a hole to develop before having them resoled. Many shoes require only a half-sole, though replacing the entire sole will make the shoe look more like new. Having new soles put on can add years of life to a shoe. A quality shoe can be resoled over and over again.

CAUTION: A shoe that is resoled can come back from the repair shop narrower than normal. If this is not what you want, make sure to tell the repairman.

Also note that shoes whose sole and upper are made from one piece of material are impossible to resole.

A synthetic sole, although less expensive than leather and perhaps more durable, is not as good. It isn't as porous, flexible, or as comfortable as a leather sole. Many women complain that they feel the balls of their feet burn in shoes made with man-made soles.

Crepe soles are fairly simple to resole (as well as reheel). You can even replace the rubber tips and heel of an espadrille.

Toe pieces. Shoe repairmen are often asked to resole the entire shoe when all that's needed is a new piece of leather to replace the worn tip of the sole, usually at half the cost.

Rubber half-soles. These serrated rubber soles, adhered to the outsole of your shoes, are a great idea if you walk on hard pavements or if your feet need extra cushioning. They also give your shoe much better traction.

Shorten the sole. If your toes don't quite come up to where they should be in an open-toe shoe, you may want to take them to a repair shop and have them cut off the excess sole that extends beyond your toes.

Sole separation. Shoe uppers can separate from the sole. This is most likely to happen with soles that are cemented to the upper, crepe-soled shoes, and shoes that were bought too tight. Once this happens, it can occur over and over again and may not be able to be fixed, but it's worth a try.

Sock Linings. When you begin to see the leather sock linings of your shoes curl up, crack, darken, or dry out, it's time to have them replaced—these can be a breeding ground for bacteria and a source of shoe/foot odor.

Squeaky Shoes. How easy are annoying squeaks to fix? It may take the repairman some time to find them, but he usually can.

Strap Alterations. A strap can be added, removed, lengthened, or shortened. A repairman can also replace the buckle attachment with a piece of elastic so you can get in and out of your shoes without having to constantly buckle and unbuckle them.

Stretching a Shoe. An experienced repairman can stretch many shoes and boots enough to make them more comfortable. (See pages 25–28 for specific guidelines regarding what can and cannot be stretched.)

CAUTION: Don't try using a shoe stretcher yourself. If your shoes need to be stretched a lot, take them to an expert. In addition to having all the right equipment, shoe repairmen routinely stretch shoes and understand well the tolerances of certain leathers and styles. Because of their experience, they are less likely to damage your shoes.

Toe Taps, Heel Plates. These are curved metal or synthetic (nylon) reinforcements that are attached to the shoe. Toe taps keep the front end of the shoe from scuffing and heel taps keep the heel lift from wearing down so quickly.

Some man-made soles, crepe soles, and open-toe shoes with thin leather soles may not be able to have taps or plates put on them.

Removing Wrinkles from a Leather Upper. A good repairman can take a leather shoe whose upper has a wrinkle or bubble in it and, by using dry heat, shrink the leather to smooth out any wrinkles.

Boot Repairs.
Most shoe repairmen can
- Raise the instep.
- Stretch the calf (usually up to 1″ or 1½″).
- Replace or *add* a zipper.

- Taper the shaft to fit women with thin calves.
- Add a gusset to accommodate a large calf.
- Cut down the height of the boot.

DYEING SHOES

Shoes can be dyed to change the color or to restore the shoe to its original color when it is so badly scuffed that polishing doesn't work anymore.

Dyeing a leather shoe properly is something only a handful of shoe-repair shops can do well. Most anybody can tint a fabric shoe, but leather dyeing is an art.

In addition to dyeing, there is refinishing. The difference between them is that in dyeing, the shoe's original finish is stripped so the new color will take. An undercoat is applied and then the shoe is dyed. A shoe that is refinished has a top coat sprayed over the original finish. Although quicker, easier, and less expensive, the finish isn't as good, nor does it last as long.

Many times a repairman will suggest that a shoe be dyed only where the finish has been stained or scuffed. Touching up a particular area of the shoe usually lasts longer than dyeing the entire shoe.

Tips to Assure Yourself of a Successful Dye Job

- Shoes can only be dyed *darker* than the original color.
- The lighter the original color of the leather the easier the job will be and the better it will come out.
- Try to stay in the same color family.
- Synthetics and suedes are very difficult to dye.

Unfortunately, most shoes that are dyed never come out as good as the original finish. Even after all the proper steps have been taken and the shoe is exactly the way you want it, the finish may scratch off easily. Additionally, the upper of a worn shoe contains perspiration and dirt, which will affect the shoe's ability to accept a dye.

Difficult Repairs That Not Every Shop Can Do

Dyeing Suede Shoes. Most shoe-repair shops don't like to dye suede because the nap tends to mat down—with some areas ending up shinier than others—and the dye is likely to bleed through later on.

Shank Repairs. Changing the height of a heel more than a lift or so may require that the shank be changed, too. Many shoe repairmen just won't do this type of work.

Molded Shoes. Shoes with heels and soles that are molded as one piece are almost impossible to work with since they cannot be taken apart like a shoe whose parts have been assembled. Most shoe repairmen consider working on these shoes a waste of your time and money and won't accept this type of work.

Relining an Entire Shoe. Most shoe-repair shops will reline parts of a shoe, the quarter or vamp, for instance, but won't reline an entire shoe. This can cost more than buying a new shoe.

Relasting a Shoe, Making It Longer. This is a repair few shops will consider doing.

Strap Repairs. If your sandals have thin straps that are coming apart at the seams, you may have a difficult time finding someone to fix them for you. Many won't even bother cementing them back together but would rather make new straps instead.

UNUSUAL REPAIRS THAT ONLY A FEW SHOPS CAN DO

In addition to normal repairs, skilled repairmen do some repairs that border on major surgery!

- Opening up the heel area on a pump and adding a strap, thus making the shoe into a slingback.
- Replacing or adding a toe cap with new or different color leather.
- Opening up the toe area on a closed-toe shoe.
- Replacing a crepe sole with a leather sole.

These repairs can be expensive, but if you want to change the look of your shoes, it may be worth doing if you can find the right repair shop to do them for you.

A Few Miscellaneous Shoe Repair Tips

- Just because one repair shop says it can't do a job doesn't mean it can't be done. Try another shop or two before giving up.
- Ask to see an example of the work a shop has done for somebody else before you leave your shoes.
- After a shoe has been repaired, it should have a neat appearance. All nicks and marks should be taken out, nails should be cut and flattened. There should be no leftover glue. Your shoes should look neat and finished.

ACKNOWLEDGMENTS

I wish to gratefully acknowledge the help of the following individuals who unselfishly gave their time, expertise, advice, and encouragment to this project.

Dr. David L. Andrews, Lisa Barsky, Dan Berk, Bill Bischoff, Dr. Harriet Blumencranz, Maria Bottino, Mr. Charles F. Brannock, Louis G. Buttell, Bob Cardone, Frank Cardone, Dr. Maurice Carter, Tony Casanova, Vidal Centeno, David H. Cohen, Richard Cohen, Bruce Colfin, Dr. Joseph C. D'Amico, Mark Darrah, Lauren Dong, Vicky Enteen, Stan Feder, Dr. Jerry Ferragamo, Lowell Feuer, Howard Fox, Harold Gessner, Richard Grabel, Dr. Bruce Heller, Glenn Herna, Irving Hertz, Michael Kamen, Mike Kormos, Victor La Hood, Helen Lo, Holly Lowe, Imre Nemuth, Sonny Onish, Mary Powers, Karen Reynolds, Anne Richter, Joe Rocco, Sr., Joe Rocco, Jr., Andrea Rosen, Dr. Bernard Rosenstein, Robert Serling, Dr. Howard Sichel, Anthony Silva, Nancy Suhre, Ralph Sutherland, Michael Svoboda, Marianne Tater, Dr. John F. Waller, Jr., Danell Wakefield—and especially to my editor, Erica Marcus, for recognizing the importance of a book like this.